NEW FIRST CERTIFICATE ENGLISH
Book 4

Listening Comprehension and Interview

W S Fowler, J Pidcock and R Rycroft

Nelson

Thomas Nelson and Sons Ltd
Nelson House   Mayfield Road
Walton-on-Thames   Surrey KT12 5PL

51 York Place
Edinburgh EH1 3JD

Thomas Nelson (Hong Kong) Ltd
Toppan Building 10/F
22A Westlands Road
Quarry Bay   Hong Kong

Distributed in Australia by

Thomas Nelson Australia
480 La Trobe Street
Melbourne   Victoria 3000
and in Sydney, Brisbane, Adelaide and Perth

© W S Fowler, J Pidcock and R Rycroft 1984

First published by
Thomas Nelson and Sons Ltd 1984

ISBN 0-17-555538-9

NPN 987

Typeset by
H Charlesworth & Co Ltd, Huddersfield

Printed and bound in Great Britain by
Scotprint Ltd., Musselburgh

Contents

Introduction

● Changes in the examination syllabus

New First Certificate English, Book 4 covers the areas of Paper 4 Listening Comprehension and Paper 5 Interview in the Cambridge First Certificate in English examination and takes into account all the changes proposed in the new 1984 syllabus.

The changes can be summed up as follows:

Paper 4: Listening Comprehension

1 There will be a series of *recorded* texts.

2 Questions will be of varying kinds, *not limited to multiple choice*, and will make use of a combined question paper/answer sheet.

3 The test will carry a final total of 20 marks out of the whole examination total of 180 marks.

4 The texts will include radio-type sequences, situational dialogues, announcements, etc. Mildly non-standard accents will be used.

5 The use of recorded material signifies a move away from the literature-oriented texts of the 1975 syllabus towards authentic spoken English in a variety of realistic contexts.

Paper 5: Interview

1 The photograph-based conversation has been retained.

2 The reading-aloud exercise has been modified. In the interview the candidate will be given a booklet containing a series of passages, asked to look at a particular one, and given a few moments to prepare to identify the speech situation in which it might occur and to discuss it.

3 The third part contains a variety of possibilities, including role-play, giving definitions or opinions, giving short talks on prepared topics, discussing how to solve specific problem situations, and, if the candidates have been studying the optional texts, discussing (or giving talks about) them.

● The design of the course

The four books comprising the *New First Certificate English* course can be used independently to concentrate on a specific paper in the examination, but they have been written in such a way that they relate to each other. The first unit of *Book 1*, for example, is devoted to descriptions of people; the first passage of *Book 2* compares a publisher's imaginary picture of authors he has never met with the reality, when they actually arrive; and the first unit in *Book 4* contains radio missing-persons messages, after which students are required to match the descriptions they have heard with a selection of photographs.
In *Books 1* and *2*, Units 5, 11, 17 and 23 are concerned with the writing and reading of narrative, and Units 6, 12, 18 and 24 with the optional literary texts; since the 1984 syllabus states that the Listening Comprehension paper will move away from literature-oriented texts, we have not linked the above units to any in *Book 4*. The table below shows how the 16 teaching units in *Book 4* relate to units in *Books 1* and *2*.

Book 4	Books 1 and 2
1	1
2	2
3	3
4	4
5	7
6	8
7	9
8	10
9	13
10	14
11	15
12	16
13	19
14	20
15	21
16	22

We have tried to make this relationship loose enough to avoid monotony, but close enough for students to be able to practise and reinforce any language or skills they have used in the linked units in the other books.

● **The contents of *Book 4***

Each of the 16 teaching units in Book 4 (intended to occupy $1\frac{1}{2}$ class hours) is divided into Listening and Speaking sections and contains:

Listening
Pre-listening activity: This is intended to allow students a few minutes to talk in a context related to the listening task that follows.

Exercise 1: This is generally a fact-based, functionally-oriented task (e.g. taking note of some information/filling in a simple form, etc.).

Exercise 2: This is generally longer and more complex than Exercise 1, requiring students to gather information by inference or interpretation as well as by 'straight' comprehension.

Speaking
Questions on the photographs and related topics: Our experience has taught us that photo contrasts, which we used in the original *First Certificate English, Book 5*, give more food for thought and produce better results in the classroom than single photographs, but in this book we have varied the approach, occasionally using one photograph and occasionally more than two.

Speech situation: A short passage, linked to the theme of the unit, is followed by questions which help to put the passage in context.

Role-plays/definitions/short talks, etc: A variety of communicative activities have been included, some requiring individual preparation and some group work. The first listening exercise in several of the units lends itself to follow-up role-play, and other activities.

Finally, there are two test units, which contain material with no thematic link.

Notes to the student

If you are preparing for the First Certificate in English examination, you should remember that neither the Listening Comprehension nor the Interview are anything to get nervous about. Here below are a few suggestions to help you.

Paper 4: Listening comprehension

1 Make sure you know exactly what you are supposed to do in each exercise. If you have any doubts, don't hesitate to ask.

2 In the examination, you will hear each recorded text twice, and you will have time to refer to the questions before (to prepare) and after each listening. With the practice exercises in this book, try to get accustomed to recognising quickly from the questions the type of information you are being asked to listen for.

3 Listening exercises are not a test of your hearing, but of your ability to understand spoken English. You should be able to hear the tape as well as you hear your radio at home. If you can't, tell your teacher. If you can't and you're in the exam, act quickly, and tell the examiner or a monitor.

4 The first time you hear a text, train yourself to listen only, without trying to answer the questions, so that you can get a clear general idea of what it is about. After the first hearing, answer as many questions as you can, but remember you also have time after the second hearing.

5 Answer *all* the questions, even if you have to guess. Blank spaces don't get marks!

Paper 5: Interview

1 Memorise the appropriate vocabulary for talking about photographs. Look at the following labelled photograph. Train yourself to be observant with photos, to study the subject of the picture as well as its physical details. Ask yourself as you look why the photographer chose *that* particular frame, and train yourself to imagine what would be visible *outside* it.

2 Read the passage through. Think about who is talking and in what situation. You will only be given a few moments to do this in the exam, so get used to doing it quickly and effectively. The examiner will first ask you a few questions to see if you have understood the context of the passage, and will then discuss it with you.

3 In the third part of the interview, since there are a variety of possibilities, make doubly sure that you know exactly what you have to do before you start. If you have been studying the prescribed books, for example, you may be asked to give a short talk about one of them, or discuss one. Or you may equally well be asked to do one of the general activities, like playing a role in a situation, or giving a definition of something (for example, an electric iron), or suggesting a solution to a problem situation, etc. Whatever the exercise, don't try to be too imaginative; work within your limits; use language you know you can use well.

4 Train yourself to converse without waiting for questions, and remember useful expressions like the following:
I'm sorry?/Pardon?/Would you mind repeating that?/I didn't quite catch what you said (if you don't understand something); and
Well/let me see/you know/you see , which, if used *appropriately*, can help you find time to think of what you are going to say next.

Lastly, we should like you to think of this book not only as a preparation for an examination, but also as a help towards developing your ability to understand spoken English and speak it yourself.

● **Acknowledgements**

Thanks are due to the following for permission to reproduce photographs:

VRU (Thomas Nelson) Introduction, pp. 2, 6 (A, C, E), 39–40, 43 (1, 2), 72   Network pp. 3 (1, 2), 11 (1), 15 (2), 19 (2), 23 (1), 47 (1), 51 (1, 2), 55 (2), 59 (1)   Villas Italia p. 6 (D)   Keystone Press pp. 7 (1, 2), 23 (2), 47 (2), 63 (1, 2)   S. and R. Greenhill pp. 11 (2), 15 (1), 27 (1, 2), 31, 35, 48 (3), 55 (1), 59 (2)   BBC Hulton Picture Library pp. 17 (A, D, E, G, H), 19 (1)   Mansell Collection p. 17 (B, C, F)   Rex Features p. 68

Every effort has been made to trace owners of copyright and if any omissions can be rectified the publishers will be pleased to make the necessary arrangements.

People

Listening

● **Pre-listening activity 1 — pair work**

Find out from your partner if he/she has had any unusual experiences in meeting people in stations, airports, etc. Find out if he/she has ever had the experience of mistaking a person for someone else.

● **Exercise 1**

You work as a courier/hostess in an international conference centre. Today it's your job to see off eight delegates from the last conference. But there's an electrical fault in the airport information boards, and you have to listen for announcements of flight numbers, departure times and boarding gate numbers. You will hear an airport announcer giving information about flights on the loudspeaker system. Complete the following table with the information you hear.

DELEGATE	DESTINATION	FLIGHT NUMBER	DEPARTURE TIME	BOARDING GATE
Mr. Suzuki	Tokyo			
Mr. Moon	Singapore			
Mr. Narayan	Nairobi			
Mr. Ben-Hadj	Muscat			
Mrs. Campesi	Rome			
Dr. Hassan	Karachi			
Dr. Mellert	Hamburg			
Dr. Kostaki	Athens			

● Pre-listening activity 2

1 Class work

Take it in turns to walk round the room, observing the other people in the class: their dress, colour of shoes, hair, eyes, etc. Then stop and stand back to back with the person nearest you. In turn, describe each other's appearance *without turning round*. The person who is being described should neither confirm nor reject what the person describing him/her says, but may ask for a more detailed description, e.g. 'Is my sweater dark or light blue?' When you have finished, turn round and compare your descriptions with the reality.

2 Pair work

Take it in turns to describe the physical appearance of a famous person *without mentioning the person's name*. See if your partner can *guess who* you are describing. The partner can ask questions to find out details.

● Exercise 2

You will hear some police messages about missing people broadcast on a local radio station. Make notes about the physical appearance and dress of the missing people. Then match your descriptions with three of the people in the photographs below. Give reasons for your choice.

Speaking

● **Questions on the photographs**

Photograph 1

1 What can you see in the picture? Describe the place. Where do you think it is? Why?
2 Describe the child, his clothing, his expression.
3 Can you see anybody else? Any children?
4 What do you think he is thinking?
5 What has he got? Where did he get it? What's he going to do with it?
6 What do you think he's been doing all morning?
7 What's he going to do now?
8 What do you think the photographer said to him?

Photograph 2

1 What can you see? Describe the place. Guess where it is and give your reasons.
2 Describe the person, clothes, expression, posture.
3 Why is she sitting like that?
4 What problems do you think she has? How does she solve them?
5 Do you think she is talking to the cat? Why?

Both photographs

1 What would these two do and say to each other if they met?
2 What would they have in common?
3 (*Pair work*) Act out a short conversation between the two people.

● Related topics

1 Why do children find it easy to get on with very old people?
2 The importance of the family as a unit. What happens to old people when the family as a unit ceases to have importance?
3 How can people best prepare to meet the problems of old age?
4 Can you imagine being very old yourself? Why is it so difficult?
5 Do you know anyone who is lonely? What can be done to help?
6 Have you ever felt completely lonely?
7 Imagine you have a very old person living in your family. Some members of the family want to send this person to an old people's home, and others want to keep him/her at home. What form would the argument take?

● Speech situation

Look through this short speech, answer the questions that follow and then discuss it.

No, he's not what you're expecting at all. It's strange you know, but everybody, absolutely everybody, expects him to be a bald, boring-looking person in a grey suit, probably with a grey tie and grey eyes, sort of *all* grey, in fact, but I'm sure you'll get a surprise when you see him. He's simply not like that.

1 Where do you think this situation is taking place?
2 What sort of person is suggested by the description?
3 Why is the word 'grey' used so often?
4 Why might everybody expect this person to be as he is described in the passage?

● Role-play — group work

Look back to Exercise 1 in the Listening section of this unit. One of you takes the role of the courier/hostess and the others are the delegates anxious not to miss their flights. The delegates should try to find out their flight departure details from the courier.

● Interpretation

Work in groups of three. Each person should first think silently of a possible interpretation of the following situation, and then compare his/her interpretation with those of the other two.

A well-dressed, attractive, middle-aged woman is sitting alone in an airport waiting area, surrounded by luggage. A teenage girl approaches the area, sees the woman, hesitates for a moment as if surprised, and then goes quickly to a public phone to make a call.

Accommodation

Listening

● **Pre-listening activity — pair work**

Find out from your partner about his/her opinions about holidays. Describe to each other your favourite type of holiday and the kind of holiday you wouldn't like. Talk about amusing experiences that have happened to you when on holiday.

● **Exercise 1**

You are going to hear a telephone conversation between a travel agent and a customer who wants to book a holiday. The travel agent asks the customer for some information about himself. Complete the form below with the information you hear.

BOOKING FORM

Holiday no.	Departure date	Number of nights

Passengers names

Mr Mrs Miss Ms	Initials	Surname	Nationality	Date of Birth if under 18	Holiday Insurance

Address of first person named to whom all correspondence will be sent, or agents stamp

Phone (Home)   (Office)

Destination/tour

Hotel/s

Rooms	Standard	Superior	Studio Apt	One Bedroom Apt	Two Bedroom Apt
Single					
Double					
Triple					
Other					

Meal plan	Room only	Room & Breakfast	Half Board	Full Board

Other requirements
- Car Hire
- Optional Tours
- Connecting Flights

PLEASE MAKE CHEQUE PAYABLE TO 'PHOENIX HOLIDAYS LTD'

You will hear two telephone conversations between a travel agent and two different customers who want to rent holiday homes. The travel agent asks the customers for information about the sort of home they require. Complete the following table with the information you hear. Then decide which two of the photographs of holiday homes the travel agent is talking about. Give reasons for your choice.

	CUSTOMER 1	CUSTOMER 2
Dates required		
No. of bedrooms		
No. of bathrooms		
No. of other rooms		
Swimming pool?		
Maid service?		
Car rental weekly		
Air fare included?		
Cost per person		

A

B

C

D

E

F

Speaking

● **Questions on the photographs**

Photograph 1

1 Describe the house in this picture.
2 Where do you think it is? How do you know?
3 What do you think there is near the house that you can't see? Why?
4 Do you notice anything unusual about the picture?
5 What's the object in front of it?

Photograph 2

1 Describe the picture. What can you see in the background?
2 What is the water for? What are the islands?
3 Can you guess where this is?
4 Can you imagine the interior of one of the flats and describe it?

Both photographs

1 What problems of maintenance would each place produce?
2 What would it be like to live in either of these two places?
3 What would be the advantages and disadvantages of each one?
4 (*Pair work*) Interview one of the occupants of either place.
5 Which would you rather live in? Why?

● **Related topics**

1 What sort of factors influence your choice of home? Put the following in order of importance.

  Memories of childhood
  5 Educational facilities
  6 Identity with area
  Sports facilities
  1 Central heating
  Tradition
  8 Neighbours
  Fireplace
  2 Cost
  3 Work
  7 Family
  Leisure
  4 Shops
  Cinemas
  Libraries
  Garden

2 What sort of life do the occupants of these various places have?
3 Describe the place you live in at the moment. Why do you live there?
4 Which building offers the most attractive architecture?
5 Why has architecture changed so much since the 1950s?

● **Speech situation**

Look through this short speech, answer the questions that follow and then discuss it.

And the place we went to last year! You can't imagine how awful it was! Of course they said it would all be perfectly clean, but you know what they're like. When we got there, it looked as if a tribe of monkeys had been camping there! Or pigs. Awful, it was.

1 What place is being referred to?
2 How does the speaker feel about it?
3 Who is talking to whom?

● **Role-play — pair work**

Look back to Exercise 1 in the Listening section of this unit. One of you takes the part of the travel agent and the other that of the customer. The customer wants to change the departure date, type of room, meal plan, etc. Act out the dialogue that might take place between them.

● **Problem situation**

Work in groups of three. You are three friends on holiday together in a rented flat. One day you find you have locked yourselves out. It is late in the evening, and there are not many other people staying in the block. Each person should suggest a solution, and the group should discuss the pros and cons of each one and decide which is the best.

Work and study

Listening

● **Pre-listening activity — group work**

Find out if any of the group have attended a course in any subject recently, and if so talk about his/her experience. If not, talk about the sort of course you would like to attend: where, how long, in what subject, etc.

● **Exercise 1**

You are going to hear a telephone conversation in which an English teacher in Milan enquires about language courses at a school in England on behalf of some Italian friends. Complete the notepad below with the information you hear.

HOW LONG? 3 OR 4 WEEKS

DATES? (MUST BE JULY)

HOW MANY CLASSES PER WEEK?

COST OF COURSE PER PERSON

TUITION?

ACCOMMODATION?

POCKET MONEY, MEALS, etc.

TOTAL COST PER PERSON?

IS ACCOMMODATION NEAR SCHOOL?

ACCOMMODATION IN FAMILIES?

● **Exercise 2**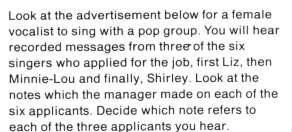

Look at the advertisement below for a female vocalist to sing with a pop group. You will hear recorded messages from three of the six singers who applied for the job, first Liz, then Minnie-Lou and finally, Shirley. Look at the notes which the manager made on each of the six applicants. Decide which note refers to each of the three applicants you hear.

VOCALISTS WANTED

26p a word

Female vocalist with professional attitude required for band, with exceptional work abroad starting 27th April. — Phone Hemel Hempstead (0442) 49933 or Harpenden (05 827) 5561.

1. Far too neurotic and too keen on money.

2. Not our type, I think. Too young and not enough good experience.

3. With this one it sounds as if her mother wants the job as much as she does. Maybe call her mother?

4. Too crazy for my taste. And — seriously — sounds too old.

5. That's better. I like her voice. Maybe not strong enough for rock?

6. She sounds too confident, too actressy for my liking. A bit too experienced.

Now listen to the piece again. Look at the following statements about each of the three applicants for the job and say whether they are true or false.

1 Liz has been told by her doctor to relax after a difficult job.
2 Liz has had no experience of singing with rock groups.
3 Minnie-Lou tries to make herself sound older than she really is.
4 Minnie-Lou is a schoolgirl who's dreaming of being a big star.
5 Shirley has probably got the most varied experience of the three.
6 It seems Shirley's parents don't want her to sing in a rock group.

10

Speaking

● **Questions on the photographs**

1 Describe what you can see in each picture.
2 Describe the men's clothing, surroundings, facial expression and posture.
3 What sort of job does each man have?
4 What sort of qualities are required for each job?
5 What sort of conditions does each have to work in? (Safety/comfort/health)
6 Do the expressions on their faces reveal anything about their attitude to work?
7 (*Pair work*) Interview one of the men about the work he does.
8 Which of these two men might earn more money? Why?

● Related topics

1 What is the relationship between pay and social importance of the job done?
2 People go to work for various reasons. Which do you think are the most important reasons? Put the following in order of importance.

    Earning a living
    Security for the future
    Meeting people
    Making a lot of money
    Getting out of the house
    Social status
    Power
    Creativity
    Satisfaction
    Travel

3 Why do you work (if you do)? Why don't you work (if you don't)?
4 Explain why people are paid the amount they are paid for the work they do. Why do footballers earn more than nurses? Why do film stars earn more than university teachers? Why do airline pilots earn more than train drivers? Who earns most in your experience? Who should?
5 If you could have any job you wanted, what would you choose, and why?
6 Do you think it's a good idea to change careers every so often, or to spend your whole life in the same career?
7 Have you ever been unemployed against your will? Talk about it.
8 In what circumstances, if any, should women be accorded different treatment from that accorded to men? Should children ever be allowed to work? Why? Why not? Should there be an age limit?

● Speech situation

Look through this short speech, answer the questions that follow and then discuss it.

They're going to concentrate on your weak points, so be prepared. Have your answers ready. And remember, they don't like people just to sit there as if they were made of wood. What they want is for you to show some interest in their side of things as well. I mean, come forward, come out of yourself a bit ... show a bit of your personality. Talk to them ... you know the sort of thing.

1 What does this passage refer to?
2 What advice does it give?
3 Who do you think is giving this advice and to whom?

● Role-play — pair work

Look back to Exercise 1 in the Listening section of this unit. Act out the dialogue that might take place between someone wanting information about the courses in the school where you are studying and the person giving that information. Use the questions on the notepad in your book where they are suitable.

● Talking point

Work in groups of three. Each person should first think silently of the job he/she would *least* like to do and the one he/she would *most* like to do, and make brief notes about them under the headings: PAY, ADVANTAGES, DISADVANTAGES. Then the group should compare their chosen likes and dislikes.

Social customs

Listening

● **Pre-listening activity — pair work**

Talk to your partner about your memories of school-, family-, children's parties, etc. Try to remember things like: the people there, time of day, food and drink, music and dancing, atmosphere.

● **Exercise 1** 🔲

Listen to these people talking about the things they need for their daughter's birthday party. Look at the following pictures of various objects and put a tick against the objects they need to buy for the party.

You are sitting in a pub near a pay-phone and hear a man called Tony Baynham making a series of phone calls to invite people to a house-warming party he and his wife, Jane, are giving the following Saturday. You will hear Tony's side of the conversation only. Listen to the way he invites the person, and say which of the people listed below he is talking to in each conversation.

a) A rather shy man.
b) Someone with intellectual/political interests.
c) A snob.
d) A person he doesn't like very much.
e) His boss.

Work in pairs and try to match the invitations with a person above.

Now listen to each conversation again and imagine what the other person says in reply to Tony.

Speaking

● **Questions on the photographs**

1 Describe each picture in detail.
2 Where do you think each picture was taken? How do you know?
3 What are the people wearing? Any clues as to social roles?
4 What does their posture and expression tell you about their relationships?
5 What do you think they are saying at the moment the photo is being taken?
6 Guess what these people normally do on a typical day in their life.
7 Can you make any guess as to what these people are doing?
8 Do you think the two pictures might be related in some way? How?
9 Look again at photograph 2. What do we understand from the following?
   a) The mouth of the lady in the white hat.
   b) The look in the man's eyes.
   c) The lady in the white hat's right hand.
   d) The man's arms.
   e) The lady in the black hat's left hand.
   f) Which hands are they each using to hold their glasses?

1

2

15

● Related topics

1 Why do people who never usually go to church insist on being married in one?
2 When else do such people go to church?
3 Do they normally drink a lot at such times? Is there a relation?
4 What sort of things do people usually talk about at weddings?

● Speech situation

Look through this short speech, answer the questions that follow and then discuss it.

I really put my foot in it, you know, and all because of you. I've never been so embarrassed in my life. I mean, it was you who told me to look out for the man with the yellow tie, because he always breaks something wherever he goes. And when he came in, the man with the yellow tie, I was standing there with a very nice girl I'd just been introduced to, you know, trying to make conversation. And I laughed, and said to her, directly to her, 'That man over there with the yellow tie is one of those awkward people who break things wherever they go.' And she said, quite coolly, 'Oh, does he? That's my father.'

1 Where do you think this situation is taking place?
2 Why was the speaker embarrassed?
3 Where was the speaker when the embarrassing incident took place?

● Role-play — pair work

Suppose you and your partner share a flat. You have invited a few friends to dinner. The one who was supposed to do the shopping for the evening meal can not get to the shops because he/she has extra work to do at the office. He/she telephones the other to ask him/her to buy all that is necessary.

● Problem situation

Work in groups of three. You are friends who share a flat, and you are giving a party. Firstly, animals are banned in the block and one of your guests has come with his dog; secondly, though it is still early, the neighbours upstairs are already protesting about the noise. Discuss possible solutions to these two problems, thinking about the advantages and disadvantages of each suggestion.

Memories

Listening

● **Pre-listening activity — pair work**

Talk about clear memories you have of things
that happened to you in your childhood, or
photographs you remember from the family
album, or stories your grandparents told you.

● **Exercise 1**

You are going to hear a grandmother talking
about some photographs from her album. Look
at the eight photographs below. Number them
1–8 in the order in which they are mentioned.

Listen to this conversation between a couple in a restaurant. They are talking about the first time they went to the restaurant twenty years before. Look at the table below and complete the first column with things which Beryl remembers of that first evening.

Then listen to the conversation again and complete the second column with things which Stanley remembers of that first evening.

	Beryl's memory	Stanley's memory
Where was the table?	In corner near window	in the corner near the band
Memory of the waiter?	Mario away - flu, flirt Young - Trevor - dark hair, tall, good voice	Mario - same waiter helpful. Trevor - stutter - black teeth
Colour of her dress?	green	long dark red
Colour of handbag?	brown	golden
Where was she sitting?	next to each other	opposite
Colour of her belt?	brown	golden
Colour of her hair?	Blonde	dark
Length of her hair?	Short	long, straight
Anything about her skin colour?	pale	suntanned dark brown
What was their own special song?	Under the Bridges of Paris	Night & Day F. Sinatra
What sort of shoes was she wearing?		High heels
What happened in the end?	Thinking another woman	

18

Speaking

● **Questions on the photographs**

Photograph 1

1 Describe this picture.
2 Can you identify what the various children are doing?
3 What other games could they be playing in the street?
4 What sort of clothes are they wearing?
5 Where and when do you think this picture could have been taken? Why?

Photograph 2

1 Describe this picture.
2 Describe the expression on the boy's face.
3 Where is he running? What from? Why?
4 What gives the picture a particularly horrific atmosphere?

1

2

Both photographs

1 What games do you remember playing as a child?
2 What things do you remember being frightened by?
3 Describe the place you lived in as a child.
4 Which of these photographs reminds you most of your childhood?
5 (*Pair work*) Interview one of the children from photograph 1.
6 What would you say to the child in photograph 2?

● **Related topics**

1 The use of children in industry, arts, cinema, theatre, publicity.
2 Should children be treated differently from adults? When and why?
3 Should children be protected from certain things? What and how?
4 Should boys be given different toys from girls?
5 War toys.
6 Does violence affect children? How?
7 How much television should children be allowed to watch? What kind of programmes?

● **Speech situation**

Look through this short speech, answer the questions that follow and then discuss it.

It's so easy now, isn't it? It's all done for you. You've got instruments for everything. You can even land in thick fog. Really, it's safer now than travelling by road. Far safer. Not like in my time. When I was learning, and that's 45 or so years ago now, there were instruments to *help* you, but you couldn't rely on them. I mean, one of the reasons why I'm so interested in the stars is that, you know. If we got lost, we used to find our way home at night by the stars. At least, that way we knew which direction we were going in.

1 What activity does the passage refer to?
2 What is the speaker comparing?
3 Who do you think is speaking to whom?

● **Problem situation**

Work in groups of three. You are friends who share a flat, and in the same block there is an old person living alone who needs help, but never asks for it. Suggest ways of helping the person and decide which suggestion(s) is/are the most practical.

● **Eliciting information**

Work in groups of three. Each person should think silently of a famous or familiar person, who once meant a lot to him/her so that the other two can ask questions about the appearance and personality of the person and so guess his/her identity. The questions can only be answered by YES or NO.

Finding the way

Listening

● **Pre-listening activity — pair work**

Explain to your partner how you normally come to class, and compare your routes, short cuts, etc.

● **Exercise 1**

Listen to the recorded instructions on where to find the hidden prize. Look at the map of Oxford below and trace the route to the hidden prize.

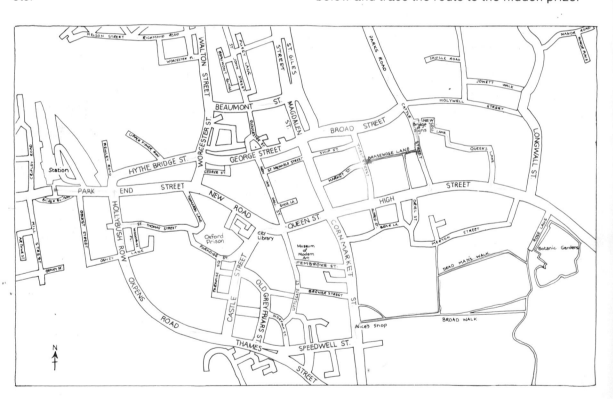

● **Exercise 2**

Listen to two friends, Mack and Greg, discussing a holiday route to take through Greece. Make notes on the special route from Patras to Athens that Mack tries to describe. DO NOT LOOK AT THE MAP YET.

After hearing the dialogue and making your notes, use them to trace Mack's route on the map. Finally, explain two possible ways of getting from the last town Mack mentions into Athens.

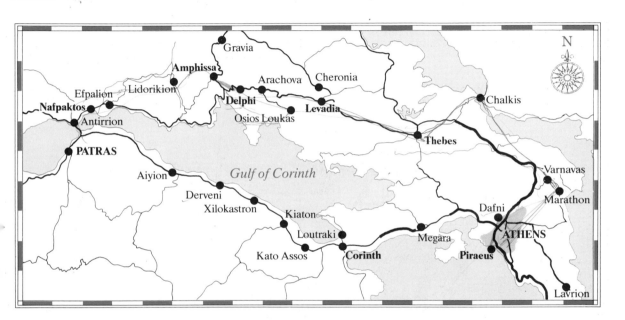

Speaking

● **Questions on the photographs**

1 Describe each one of these photographs in detail.
2 Describe the people.
3 Can you guess where each one was taken? How did you guess?
4 (*Pair work*) Interview one of the people in photograph 2.
5 Look at the scene in photograph 1. Can you imagine what happened before and after this?

6 What do you imagine the people in each photograph can hear and smell?
7 What would you feel if you were in either of these scenes?
8 Is it worth being herded around at airports to get to your destination?
9 Would you like to live in the scenery shown in picture 1? Why (not)?

1

2

● Related topics

1 What other kinds of holiday are there?
2 What kind of holiday do you prefer in the summer?
3 How important is tourism to the economy of your country?
4 Would you recommend anyone to come to your country on holiday? Why?
5 What do you think of the tourists who visit your country?
6 Do you think international tourism helps to improve international understanding?
7 Is it important to try to find out about the customs of the country you visit?
8 What's the best way of doing this?
9 Do you sometimes wish tourism had never been invented?

● Speech situation

Look through this short speech, answer the questions that follow and then discuss it.

You'll need to go prepared, of course. Once you get away from the village, out into open country, remember there's nobody ahead of you, nowhere you can go for shelter for another fifteen miles. I mean, it's really wild country, don't make any mistake about that. Very beautiful, certainly, and marvellous walking country, but wild. Even in summer you've got to watch the weather, because once the clouds come down it's easy to lose your way.

1 What activity is the speaker referring to?
2 What advice does the speaker give?
3 Who do you think the speaker is giving this advice to?

● Eliciting information

Work in groups of three. One of you lives in Oxford, somewhere on the map on page 21. The other two arrive at the railway station and phone the third to ask for directions of how to get to his/her house. The third makes a game of this and says he/she will give them ten questions each, to be answered with YES or NO, so that they can guess where he/she lives. Refer to the map.

Opinion

Listening

● **Pre-listening activity — pair work**

Find out what your partner thinks of phone-in shows on the radio, and whether he/she has heard any interesting topics discussed on one recently.

● **Exercise 1** 📼

You are now going to hear an excerpt from a phone-in programme in which the topic is a plan to enlarge an airport. *Listen only* the first time through. Then look at the following list of mistakes which the caller *could* make. Listen to the piece again and tick the mistakes that the caller *in fact* makes when he calls the programme.

a) He exaggerates the problem.
b) He makes his best point at the beginning, not the end.
c) He is too impatient with the other callers' opinions.
d) He never gets to the point.
e) He begins by apologising.
f) He does not keep to the point.
g) It seems he doesn't really know what he wants to say.
h) He allows the announcer, Molly, to put him off.
i) He is too worried about what listeners will think of him.
j) He tries to annoy Molly.

● Exercise 2　🖭

You are going to hear part of a radio programme in which an economist makes comparisons between conditions now and 25 years ago. Take notes as you listen, and then fill in the table below with the items or figures the economist mentions. Make it clear if he is talking of hours, minutes, weeks, etc.

ITEM	25 YEARS AGO	NOW
small car		
a pair of leather shoes		
	44 minutes	
		$1\frac{1}{4}$
a gas cooker		
	4	
		6 minutes
a kilo of		
	32	
		10 minutes
6		
	$10\frac{1}{2}$	

Speaking

● **Questions on the photographs**

Photograph 1

1 Describe the picture.
2 What city would you guess this is? How do you know?
3 Can you describe exactly what you can see in the foreground?
4 Who put it there, do you think? Why?
5 Who will have to clean it up?
6 How much will they be paid for cleaning it up? Who will have to pay in the end?
7 Could any of this material be used again?
8 What do you think of people who dump rubbish in the street?
9 (*Pair work*) Someone is about to dump some rubbish in the street. Ask him to reconsider.

Photograph 2

1 Describe this picture. What sort of buildings and structures are there in the background?
2 Where do you think this might be? How do you know?
3 What can you see in the middle of the picture?
4 How do you think the bicycle got there?
5 What do you think the water is like? Would there be any fish here?

● Related topics

1 How can dumping be reduced?
2 What can be done to encourage people to help recycle useful waste?
3 Should people who pollute rivers be punished? How?
4 Describe your own city. Is it clean enough? What is being done?
5 Are there any kinds of dumping that are really dangerous for the environment?
6 Do you know of any movements like GREENPEACE? What do you think of them?

● Speech situation

Look through this short speech, answer the questions that follow and then discuss it.

You can't say that! How do you know, anyway? I mean, allow me to tell you, because I'm a doctor and I know about these things. If there's one thing that makes me angry, it's when I hear people giving opinions about a medical question when they just don't know what they're talking about. You simply cannot understand the problem unless you have experience, direct experience of it, every day of your life, as I do...

1 What is the attitude of the speaker?
2 What has caused the speaker to take this attitude?
3 Where do you think this situation is taking place?

● Role-play — group work

You each have about $1\frac{1}{2}$–2 minutes to give an opinion on a phone-in radio programme, like that in Exercise 1 of the Listening section of this unit. First, agree on a topic from the following list and then, individually, prepare what you want to say in your allotted time. Those who are not speaking should take it in turns to be the programme presenter. Learn from Mr Makepeace's mistakes!

Street crime
Private and state health care
Nuclear disarmament
Cigarette advertising
The Miss World beauty contest
Using animals for research purposes

Plans and forecasts

Listening

● **Pre-listening activity — pair work**

Find out from your partner if there have been any occasions in his/her life when unexpected or bad weather caused a change of plans, or caused something unusual to happen.

● **Exercise 1**

You are going to hear a weather forecast. Look at the map of England, Wales and Scotland below. Put the appropriate symbol in each of the boxes linked to the six areas mentioned to show what sort of weather each area can expect.

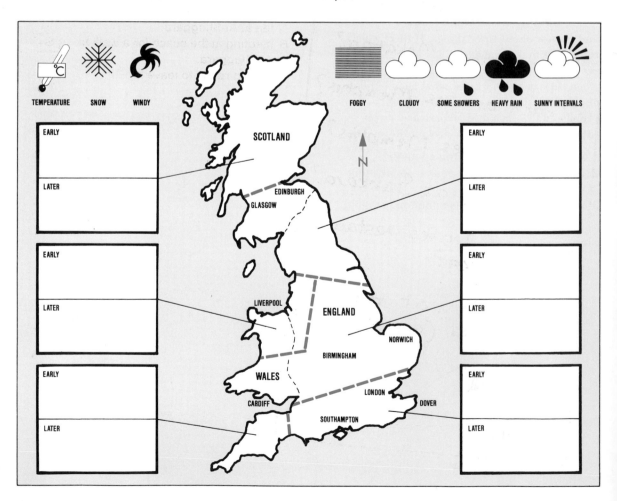

You will hear a courier explaining the day's programme to a group of tourists who are going on a day trip round Cairo, Egypt. For question 1, look at the notepad in your book and fill in the times you hear. For questions 2–4 put a tick in one of the boxes, A, B or C.

1

CAIRO / PYRAMIDS TRIP

1. Coach leaves Mokattam?

2. Coach arrives Memphis?

3. Coach leaves Memphis?

4. How long at Sakkara?

5. Coach leaves restaurant for Giza?

6. How long at the Pyramids (approx)?

2 The photographers in the group shouldn't worry about Mokattam because
   A the coach will stop on the way there to allow them to take some pictures. [A]
   B if the weather's clear the coach will stop there for them. [B]
   C there'll be an organised stop there for them to take pictures. [C]

3 The group should stay together in one area of the restaurant because
   A in that area they'll be served more quickly. [A]
   B if they sit anywhere else they won't be served. [B]
   C they'll have to pay more in any other section. [C]

4 At 4.30 the group should be
   A in the coach, waiting to leave for tea at Al-Shaggara. [A]
   B meeting at the coach for a walk to Al-Shaggara. [B]
   C getting ready to leave for Giza. [C]

Speaking

1 Describe the picture in detail. How many different types of vehicles are there?
2 Can you see any cars with room for an extra passenger?
3 Describe the pedestrian, his clothes, his way of walking.
4 What can he see, hear and smell? What might he be thinking?
5 Where might this have been taken? What clues are there to help you?
6 What could be done to solve this problem?

● Related topics

1 (*Pair work*) Ask your partner whether he/she owns a car and why.
2 Why do people buy cars when they can't afford them and don't need them?
3 How many reasons can you think of for owning a car?
4 What does owning a car mean to:
   a) a man who lives in a city?
   b) a family who live in a small market town?
   c) an old woman who lives alone in the country?
   d) a young woman with a baby and a small child?
5 What sort of car would you recommend to these people?
6 Do you know anything about car maintenance? Do you do it yourself? Why not?
7 Could you imagine a large city without cars? How would you plan it?
8 How many different sorts of people depend on the continuation of the motor industry for their livelihood?
9 Why are we still using petrol-driven cars 100 years after the invention of the petrol engine? Haven't circumstances changed since then?

● Speech situation

Look through this short speech, answer the questions that follow and then discuss it.

Well, for people under that sign it will be one of those weeks, I'm afraid, where it seems very difficult to make any progress. You know, you'll probably have your plans, but nobody will do exactly what you want, and even if they *do* do what you want, they won't do it in *the way* you want. So the best advice I can give you is 'be patient', because there are clear signs that next week's going to be a lot better.

1 What does the passage refer to?
2 Who is giving this information and advice?
3 Where else would you find this sort of advice?

● Talking point

Work in groups of three. Each person should first think silently of how he/she thinks home life will change over the next twenty years, and note down two or three ideas; the group should then discuss their opinions.

Do-it-yourself holidays

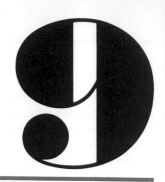

Listening

● **Pre-listening activity — group work**

Discuss your experiences of family or group excursions. How would you prefer to travel if you were going somewhere in your country next weekend — by car, bus, coach or train?

● **Exercise 1**

You are going to hear a person phone a car hire agency to enquire about hiring a car. Complete the notepad below with the information given by the clerk in the agency.

HIRE THE CAR

PHONE CANNING'S TEL. 652714
REMEMBER IT'S THE WHOLE WEEK

FIND OUT
BEST CAR FOR 4 PEOPLE AND LUGGAGE?
ESCORT £100   CORTINA £125
PICK UP AT WHAT TIME?
MONDAY MORNING.

COST
BASIC WEEKLY? £100
UNLIMITED MILEAGE OR
PAID BY THE MILE?
DEPOSIT? EVERYTHING AT THE BEGINNING of the hire
HOW MUCH FOR EXTRA DAYS? £6 per day
EXTRA FOR 2 DRIVERS? £2.50 for the week
INSURANCE INCLUDED? YES.
ANY V.A.T. TO PAY? 15%

You will hear a radio interview with an expert
on camping who gives advice on what to take
on a camping holiday. Look at the objects
pictured below and put a tick against each item
that he advises campers to take with them.

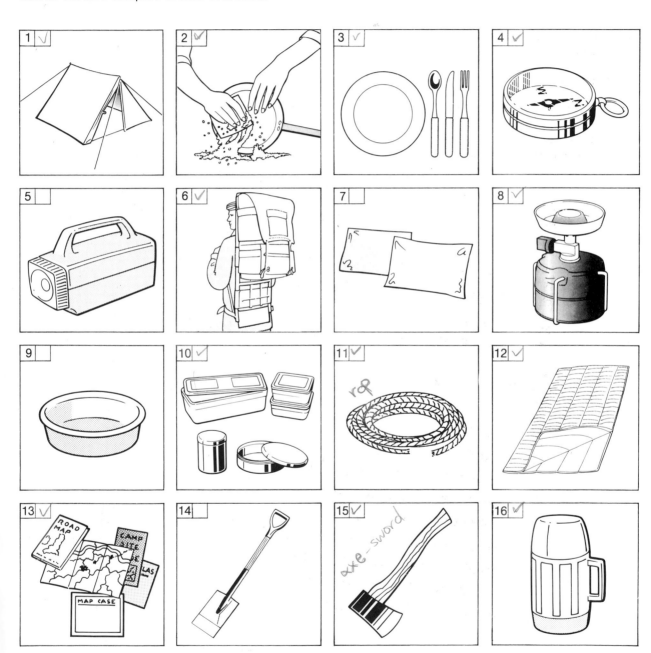

34

Speaking

● Questions on the photograph

1 Describe this picture.
2 What do you think the people are trying to do?
3 Describe in detail what each of the people is actually doing.
4 What does the child think?
5 Describe the room in detail. Have they done anything else themselves?
6 Are they doing it properly? Could you suggest some improvements in their technique?
7 Have you ever done anything like this? How did it turn out?

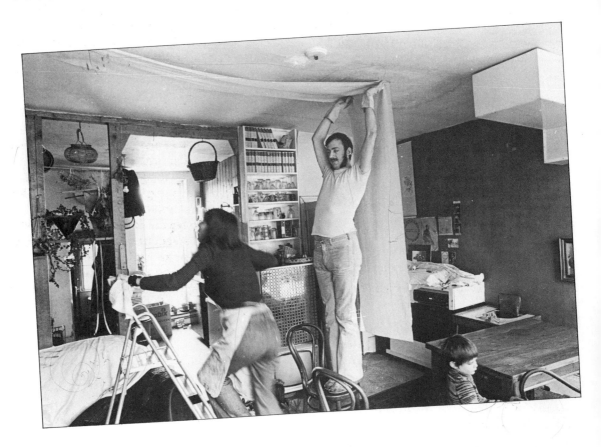

● Related topics

1 (*Group work*) In groups of four or five, find out which of you are able to do the following things by yourselves, without calling in a professional.

> Installing electrical circuits
> Painting and decorating
> Building a wall
> Servicing a car
> Making furniture
> Planting and growing flowers and plants
> Laying carpets, lino, floor tiles
> Making curtains, lampshades, cushions
> Plumbing, unblocking drains
> Making and altering clothes, knitting

Award two points for each of the above jobs that you have actually done and one point for each activity that you know how to do. Compare your results with other groups.

2 Why do people do things themselves? Is it in any way anti-social?

3 (*Pair work*) Choose any of the skills mentioned in question 1. Act out a conversation between an amateur, who starts by saying, 'Ooh, that's easy; anyone could do that!', and the professional, who answers, 'It's not as easy as it looks, you know.'

● Speech situation

Look through this short speech, answer the questions that follow and then discuss it.

No! Hold it there. Don't move! But you have! You have moved. It's not straight. The right-hand side's lower than the left. No, not that much. Raise it a bit. A bit more. That's it. No, you've let it drop again. Up a bit more. That's it. Now hold it there, tightly. Right. Now press it, hard. Let's see if it sticks.

1 Where do you think this situation is taking place?
2 Who is speaking to whom?
3 What do you think the person spoken to is doing?

● Role-play — pair work

Look back to Exercise 1 in the Listening section of this unit. Read the information below and act out the dialogue that might take place.

STUDENT A: You want to hire a car for the weekend for yourself and your husband/wife. You want to know the following from the car hire agency: cars available? time you can pick up car? and return it? cost? charge per mile? any V.A.T.? any petrol included in the price? insurance included? other drivers extra?

STUDENT B: You are the agency clerk. You have a special weekend offer of a Ford Fiesta at £33, a Ford Escort at £36 and a Ford Cortina at £40. Pick up Friday 12.00 midday, return Monday 9.00 a.m. Unlimited mileage. V.A.T. not included so add 15%. Full fuel tank start, then customer pays for petrol. Fully insured. Extra charge for second driver — £3; driver must be approved by agency.

● Explanation

Work individually at first. You are studying in a language school in Britain where it has become a tradition for students to prepare a supper on one evening during the course. The supper is a buffet and each national group contributes one typical dish. Note down what dish you would select from your country/region, with a *brief* explanation of what it is (*not* a recipe). Then find out from your partners (in groups of three) what they have suggested.

Advertising

Listening

● **Pre-listening activity — pair work**

Find out what sort of radio or television advertisements your partner likes or dislikes, and see if you can both explain why some attract you and some not.

● **Exercise 1** 🔳

Read the following critical descriptions of ten advertisements broadcast on a commercial radio station. Then listen to recordings of *six* of the adverts that you have read about. Match each of the six with one of the descriptions in your book and put the advertisement number in the appropriate box.

a How can a man be stupid enough to believe that if he uses this (cosmetic product) he'll end up alone on a desert island with a beautiful girl? I speak from bitter experience here because I've tried them all!

b Another variation on the idea 'If you've read the book which was a bestseller, you'll like the film'. Not only that, you'll be able to impress your friends (and enemies!) by saying 'Of course the film/book is *far* better than the book/film!' In spite of the ad I might go to the film.

c This one suggests that this new household product will make the things it cleans better than they were when new. It also makes the typical housewife look stupid. Very silly and (unintentionally?) comic.

d This one plays with people's fears quite humorously. It presupposes that people have seen the other, far more famous film about creatures from outer space. I don't much like horror films, but I might go to this.

e Use this medicine on your skin, this one tells young people, and you'll lose your shyness and make friends, etc. I hope it works.

f This one suggests that scientists have produced a new 'magic' solution to a common household problem. It uses the fantastic idea to make the 'typical' housewife in the story think the product will work as fast and as well as magic. And then the scientists come on at the end and tell us there are <u>real</u>, serious, scientific explanations for the magic. Probably the same old product in a different coloured tin.

g This one plays on some mothers' fears that they may not be as good as others. So the little daughter is used to make her mother guilty and anxious to use the same product as the mum next door. I'm determined not to buy the product.

h This is one for people suffering in the middle of a cold British winter. The attraction of the warm sunny south. As my holidays don't start till July 15, it made me angry, however cheap it is.

i This is another of those ads for young people which treats them as if they were born without a mind. 'I didn't know what I wanted till my friend told me about X'. I wouldn't buy this even if it was the only one in the shop!

j This one plays on people's fears of being in a foreign country without knowing the language, etc. They try to make the traveller feel that wherever he goes it will be just as safe as the street where he lives. Not my sort of holiday, but still...

● Exercise 2

Listen to the street interview on the subject of television advertisements. Look at the interviewer's questionnaire below and complete it with the information you hear.

Research Project : Television advertisements

Interviewer's No. 739

Date ....

Name of interviewee .... Age .... Sex M/F ....

Occupation ....

How many hours television per week? 0-5 ..... 6-10 ..... 11-15 ..... 16+ .....

Favourite television ads? cartoons .... with animals ... with children ...
with story-line ... informative ... amusing ...
other (please specify) ....

Does interviewee find it easy to remember television ads? YES/NO

Can he/she remember the name of any products advertised by :
1) cartoons? YES/NO   2) ads with animals? YES/NO
3) ads with children? YES/NO   4) ads with story-line? YES/NO
5) informative type of ad? YES/NO   6) others ....
....

Does he/she prefer ads with or without music? ....

Does he/she like ads with jingles/songs/repeated slogans? ....

What sort of ads does he/she dislike, and why? ....
....

Would he/she buy a product simply because he/she had seen it advertised on
television? YES/NO

If a product is advertised on television, does that suggest to him/her that the
product should be good? YES/NO

Would he/she prefer television without advertisements? YES/NO

Speaking

● **Questions on the photographs**

1 Describe each one of these advertisements in detail.
2 What do you think they are trying to sell?
3 What do you think the product really consists of?
4 Who is each advertisement aimed at?
5 Comment on the slogans used and suggest alternative slogans to go with each advertisement.
6 Could these advertisements be used to sell anything else? What?
7 Could these advertisements arguably be said to be informative?
8 Do the advertisements in any way distort or misrepresent the truth? How?
9 Do advertisements in general, and these in particular, exploit people by relying on their weaknesses? What should be done to make this more difficult?

1

2

3

4

● Related topics

1 Are advertisements in any way necessary in society?
2 Why, do you think, are advertising executives among the highest-paid people in the whole of the commercial world?
3 Is there any need for the audience to be protected from half-truths and lies? Is there any law in your country that protects the public from deliberate misrepresentation?
4 Do you think advertisements can be artistic? Do you know any examples?
5 How many different ways are there of advertising a product?
6 What are your views on 'censorship' and 'decency'?
7 Do you think it right that political parties use public relations offices to help them project a good image to the public, especially around election times?

● Speech situation

Look through this short speech, answer the questions that follow and then discuss it.

Go on. Take one. Nobody's looking. Bite into it. Bite off just a little piece. Do you feel that taste? No, don't look round. There's nobody there. Have another bite, go on. You've got time. I know, you think you shouldn't eat between meals but this is a special occasion, isn't it? And you won't be alone with that box again today. The second was even better than the first, wasn't it? Go on, have a third. You don't begin to feel the full benefit of them till you've had at least three...

1 What is the speaker encouraging the other person to do?
2 What kind of reaction does the speaker expect from the other person?
3 Where might you hear this sort of talk?

● Eliciting information

Work in groups of three. Take it in turns to think of a popular advertised product and allow your partners a maximum of twenty questions (which are answered by YES or NO) to guess the product. They must guess the function of the product, its brand name, and something about the way it is advertised.

Buying and selling

11

Listening

● **Pre-listening activity — pair work**

Find out about your partner's experience in shopping. Does he/she prefer buying things in big or small shops? Has he/she had amusing or unusual experiences in shopping? Does he/she like shopping in sales? Or in auctions? Or markets? What is his/her attitude to bargains and what was the best one he/she remembers?

● **Exercise 1**

You are going to hear two women, Mrs Trim and Mrs Morgan, talking about clothes they bought in the sales. Complete the table below with the information you hear.

ITEM	PRICE PAID BY MRS TRIM (first speaker)	ORIGINAL PRICE	PRICE PAID BY MRS MORGAN	ORIGINAL PRICE
Dress				
		£22.99		
				£20
	£8			

● **Exercise 2**

You will hear part of a radio interview about the launch of a new car.

For questions 1–4 put a tick in one of the boxes A, B, C or D. For question 5, look at the interviewer's notepad and complete it with the information you hear.

1 For the launch of the new car,
  A Madeira was not chosen because its roads were too dangerous. [A]

B the Costa del Sol was finally chosen after three months of investigation. [B]

C Britain was not chosen because snow was forecast for April. [C]

D Portugal was not chosen because it was not quiet enough for the press. [D]

2 Of the production models of the new car,
  A at least 60 had been tested on British roads by the end of the previous October. [A]

B 30 were shipped from England to Spain in containers.

C about 50 were driven from the factory to Plymouth at night.

D only 50 were tested on British roads at night.

3 The car company sent

A in all, forty technicians to the launch.

B some technicians specialised in preventing accidents.

C all the technicians overland to Marbella in six Range Rovers.

D about half as many technicians as cars to the launch.

4 The first visitors to see the car at the launch were

A the British regional press.

B the foreign press.

C the car dealers and their wives.

D correspondents from the British national press.

5

DIARY OF A £1 MILLION LAUNCH

LAST YEAR JAN?

MARCH, APRIL?
ANYTHING?

OCTOBER?

BEFORE THE END OF YEAR?

THIS YEAR   JANUARY?

WHEN DID THEY START PREPARING
THE HOTELS?
HOW MANY FROM THE NATIONAL
PRESS AND WHERE WILL THEY BE
STAYING?

NEXT WEEK? WHERE?

AFTER NEXT WEEK - WHERE?
WITH WHO?

WHEN IS PRESENTATION TO
FOREIGN PRESS?

Speaking

● **Questions on the photographs**

Photograph 1

1 What sort of things is the stall holder selling?
2 Describe how he is dressed.
3 Do you think this kind of selling is hygienic?
4 How do stall holders like this man attract their customers?
5 What is sold on market stalls in your country?

Photograph 2

1 What kinds of food can you see for sale?
2 What sort of shop do you think this is? Why?
3 Why do you think the shop assistants are wearing uniform?
4 Do you prefer to buy this kind of food as it is sold here or in plastic packages? Why?

Both photographs

1 Who do you think works harder, a market stall holder or a shop assistant? Who makes more money? What other advantages/disadvantages are there to each job?
2 What view of people do you think a stall holder or a shop assistant must get?
3 (*Pair work*) Interview either the stall holder or one of the shop assistants about their work.

● Related topics

1 Have you ever tried to sell anything? Are you good at it?
2 Would you like to be a shop assistant? If so, in what kind of shop or showroom?
3 What do you like or dislike about shopping?
4 What is your reaction when a shop assistant is rude to you, or gives you the wrong change? Do you attack, or try to understand?
5 Who usually does the shopping in your family? Why?

● Speech situation

Look through this short speech, answer the questions that follow and then discuss it.

I feel very strongly about this. I mean, the people who do all the work don't see the result of it. They don't make much of a profit at all. It's the people in the middle, the ones between the producers and the customers, who get the best out of it. The distributors, the shopkeepers, and so on. There must be a better way of organising things, so that the people who do the hard work get a better share of the profits.

1 What does the passage refer to?
2 What is the speaker's main complaint?
3 How would the speaker like to see things improved?

● Talking point

Work in groups of three. Note down your individual answers to the following two questions and then discuss them with your partners.
1 Cars are designed, made and sold by men for men.
2 The conversation we heard about sales in Exercise 1 of the Listening section is unfair to women.

Listening

● **Pre-listening activity 1 — pair work**

Find out if your partner has had any experience with football pools, has ever won anything in a lottery, etc. What would you do with the money if you did?

● **Exercise 1** 🔲

You are going to hear an excerpt from a sports programme on the radio in which a football pools forecaster predicts the results of the next set of matches to be played in Division One. Look at the pools chart below and complete the right-hand column with the forecaster's prediction. Put 'X' for a draw, '1' for a home win and '2' for an away win.

H A D 10 years	Last 5 Home Games	DIVISION 1 H	A	Last 5 Away Games	Write X, 1 or 2 here
4 — 2	W W D W W	Arsenal v	Southampton	L W D L W	
2 — —	L W D W W	Birmingham v	Swansea	D L D L D	
1 3 —	L D L D D	Brighton v	Tottenham Hotspur	D D L D W	
5 1 1	W D W W W	Ipswich v	Aston Villa	L W L L D	
2 1 —	W W W W D	Liverpool v	Sunderland	W D L W W	
1 — —	L D L D L	Luton v	Norwich	L L D L D	
3 2 3	D W D D W	Manchester United v	Coventry	D L L L D	
2 1 2	W L D L L	Nottingham Forest v	Everton	W L D L D	
1 — 2	W W L W W	Stoke v	Notts County	L W L L L	
3 3 1	L D D W W	West Bromwich Albion v	Manchester City	D L L L L	
1 — 1	L L D W D	West Ham v	Watford	L W L W L	

H = Home (i.e. the team is playing on its home ground) A = Away (i.e. the team is playing away from its home ground)
W = Won L = Lost D = Drawn

● Pre-listening activity 2

Look at the pools chart in Exercise 2. Using the
information given about each team, fill in your
pools forecast in the left-hand column. Put 'X'
for a draw, '1' for a home win and '2' for an
away win. You may need to refer to Exercise 1
for a key to the abbreviations or to look at the
results forecast on the radio sports
programme.

NOTE   In the pools chart the information is
arranged as follows:

e.g. In the last 10 years Arsenal have played at
home to Southampton 6 times. In those 6
matches, Arsenal, the Home team (H), have
won 4 times; Southampton, the Away team (A),
have not won at all, and 2 of the matches have
been drawn. Of their last 5 HOME games *this*
season, Arsenal have won 4 and drawn 1. Of
their last 5 AWAY games this season,
Southampton have won 2, lost 2 and drawn 1.
This information *may* help you to make up your
mind, but you may prefer to close your eyes
and make a guess.

● Exercise 2

You will hear an excerpt from a sports
programme in which the football results are
announced as they come in. They are from all
divisions and are not arranged in order. Look
at the pools chart below and complete the
right-hand column with the actual result. Put 'X'
for a draw, '1' for a home win and '2' for an
away win.

Your Forecast	H A D 10 years	Last 5 Home Games	DIVISION 1 H	A	Last 5 Away Games	Actual Result
	4 — 2	W W D W W	Arsenal v	Southampton	L W D L W	
	2 — —	L W D W W	Birmingham v	Swansea	D L D L D	
	1 3 —	L D L D D	Brighton v	Tottenham Hotspur	D D L D W	
	5 1 1	W D W W W	Ipswich v	Aston Villa	L W L L D	
	2 1 —	W W W W D	Liverpool v	Sunderland	W D L W W	
	1 — —	L D L D L	Luton v	Norwich	L L D L D	
	3 2 3	D W D D W	Manchester United v	Coventry	D L L L D	
	2 1 2	W L D L L	Nottingham Forest v	Everton	W L D L D	
	1 — 2	W W L W W	Stoke v	Notts County	L W L L L	
	3 3 1	L D D W W	West Bromwich Albion v	Manchester City	D L L L L	
	1 — 1	L L D W D	West Ham v	Watford	L W L W L	

Speaking

● Questions on the photographs

1 Describe each photograph in detail. Pay attention to clothes, posture, stance.
2 Can you guess where any of them were taken? How? (What clues have you got?)
3 Why do people like to dress up? What exactly are these people doing?
4 Why do you think people like pretending to be cowboys and Vikings?
5 What other ways are there for people to escape from reality for a moment?
6 Would you like to be in any one of these scenes? Which one? Why?

1

2

3

● **Related topics**

1 Have you ever been to a large amusement
park or fairground? Talk about it.
2 Have you ever been to Disneyworld or
Disneyland? Would you like to? What do you
think you would find if you went there? What
would you probably like/dislike?
3 Do you ever go to the cinema? What sort of
films do you like? Why?
4 What do you think of violence in films? Is it
just an inoffensive way of helping people to
relax, or is it something more sinister?
5 Do you know of any cartoons for children that
you find particularly disturbing?
6 Why do you think that a lot of our 'relaxing'
often involves 'letting off steam', which in
turn often involves suppressed violence?

● **Speech situation**

Look through this short speech, answer the
questions that follow and then discuss it.

And then the door opened, noisily, and, you
know, it was all dark. The girl was frightened,
naturally, because she knew, or at least she
thought, she was alone in the house. So she called
out 'Who's there?' and there was no reply. Only
silence, and the noise of the wind and the rain
outside. And then... and then... you'll never
guess what happened next...

1 What is the passage about?
2 What kind of atmosphere does the speaker
build up?
3 What kind of reaction is the speaker aiming
to produce in the listener(s)?

● **Talking point**

Work in groups of three. Choose whichever of
the following is your favourite entertainment
and note down the reasons why. Then discuss
your opinions with your partners.
Radio and television
Spectator sports
Dancing
Any others
Cinema
Theatre
Music

Where to live

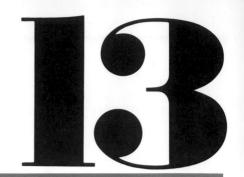

Listening

● **Pre-listening activity — pair work**

Find out from your partner his/her answers to the following questions.

*Where would you like to live: **a** in your country, if you didn't live where you do now? and **b** abroad, if you had to move from your country?*

● **Exercise 1**

Listen to this excerpt from a radio interview in which a sociologist talks about maps which children have drawn of their neighbourhood. Look at the maps below and decide which child drew each map.

A

ANNUNCIATION STREET
TRADE HIGH
PRENTIS STREET
STREET
STREET
FACTORY
PARKING LOT
STREET
WAREHOUSE
KIES STORE
EMPTY LOT
JOHNS STORE
PARKER STREET   (TREMONT STREET) →
WENTWORTH INSTITUTE
MISSION HILL PROJECT
SMITH STREET
WOOD STREET
HONTINGTON AVENUE
RENT OFFICE

B

Annunciation
Parking Lot
St. Prentis
PRENTISS St.
Cumberland farm store
savis store
other people
Drug store
PARKER STREET
Smith St.
school
Mission hill
Mission hill Project.

C

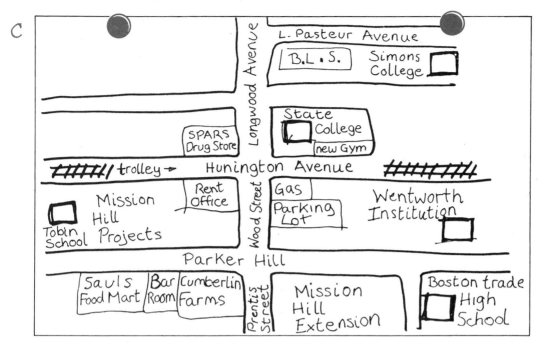

A map showing the following labelled locations: Longwood Avenue, L. Pasteur Avenue, B.L.S., Simons College, SPARS Drug Store, State College (new Gym), trolley →, Hunington Avenue, Mission Hill Projects, Rent Office, Wood Street, Gas, Parking Lot, Wentworth Institution, Tobin School, Parker Hill, Sauls Food Mart, Bar Room, Cumberlin Farms, Prentis Street, Mission Hill Extension, Boston trade High School.

● **Exercise 2**

You will hear another excerpt from the interview with the sociologist about the way people choose a place to live. Look at the following questions and tick one of the boxes A, B, C or D for each question.

1 Country life
  A makes country people feel superior to townspeople. [A]
  B annoys some townspeople because of its lack of variety. [B]
  C offers a lot of attractions which few townspeople can resist. [C]
  D lacks the services that some townspeople feel are essential. [D]

2 A place with a good climate is a natural attraction
  A except for people from countries where most houses have central heating. [A]
  B because people who live in wet climates suffer from bronchitis in winter. [B]
  C for people who are thinking of moving to a new place. [C]
  D mainly when it is a question of physical survival. [D]

3 A People living in the northern USA would never dream of going to live in the southern states like Alabama. [A]
  B People in the west have a negative impression of oriental countries. [B]
  C Eastern-bloc countries only attract people who reject the western social model. [C]
  D People don't like moving to a country that is politically unstable. [D]

4 People
  A don't like living in out-of-the-way places. [A]
  B like living in town centres. [B]
  C like living on desert islands only if they are easy to get to. [C]
  D feel attracted by life on desert islands only if they are lonely. [D]

Speaking

● **Questions on the photographs**

1 Describe each photograph in detail. Mention something about the atmosphere of each.
2 Where do you think each one was taken? How do you know?
3 What do you think you would have seen all around you if you had stood beside the photographer when he/she took each photograph? Describe the smells and sounds.
4 What sort of life do you think the farmer has? What sort of timetable does he have to follow? What is life like in the winter for him? What does his dog mean to him?
5 Look at photograph 2. What sort of place do you think this is? How do you know?
6 Describe a typical day in the life of a person who works in the place in picture 2.
7 (*Pair work*) Imagine the farmer met one of the miners in a pub. Invent a conversation in which they both talk about their work.

51

● Related topics

1 What are the advantages of living and working in the country, as compared with living and working in an industrial city?
2 Where would you rather live? Why?
3 Why do many people who live in cities long to go back to nature, while people who live in small villages want to come to the big cities?
4 Imagine you suddenly inherited a great deal of money — a complete surprise. Now where are you going to live? In which country? Which part? In what sort of house? (You can only have one residence — it is stipulated in the will.)
5 Where would you advise the following people to live and why?
   A young man who wants to be an athlete
   An elderly retired couple
   A single student who wants to study botany
   A young married couple with no children
   A family of seven who are looking for work
   A foreign student learning the language of the country he/she is living in
   A person who has just qualified as a doctor
   An art student
   A foreign journalist
   A group of young actors
6 What reasons do people usually give for living in the city? Think of a list of ten and then put them in order of importance.
7 Now do the same for reasons for living in the country.

● Speech situation

Look through this short speech, answer the questions that follow and then discuss it.

For a week or so before the festival, people pile up all sorts of things, anything you can burn... you know, old furniture, boxes and so on... in some open place in the neighbourhood. And then, on the night itself, they gather round the fires and let off fireworks. And usually they get a band to come and play for a dance afterwards. And when that's over, well, if you've got the energy, you go up the hill near the town and wait to see the sunrise.

1 What is the speaker describing?
2 What preparations do people make for this event?
3 What sort of activities do people take part in during the event?
4 Who might the speaker be describing the event to?

● Eliciting information

Work in groups of three. Take it in turns to think of a popular tradition, custom or belief in your country and allow your partners twenty questions (which you answer by YES or NO) to guess what you are thinking of.

Officialdom

Listening

● **Pre-listening activity — pair work**

In your country, what sort of reputation does your railway system have? Do trains generally arrive on time? Are they comfortable? Too crowded? Compare your experiences.

● **Exercise 1**

Listen to these train announcements. Look at the map below. In the numbered boxes beside the map write the time of the train you would have to catch to get to each destination indicated. Put a tick in the box if you would need to *change* trains in order to get to that destination.

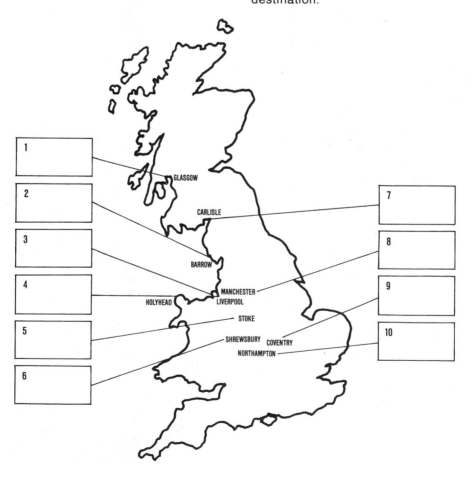

● **Exercise 2**

You will hear one side of a telephone conversation divided into five parts. Look at the questions below and tick one of the boxes A, B or C for each question. There is one question for each part of the conversation.

1 Why does the caller insist so much on the day and date?
   A She wants to make it clear that she did not register on the last possible day. ☐ A
   B She wants to prove that she did not forget to register. ☐ B
   C She did not go to register at all, but thinks she can persuade the clerk that she did. ☐ C

2 Why does the caller insist so much that nobody in the office told her about the rule?
   A She would have paid then if they had told her. ☐ A
   B She thinks her best argument is that they informed her wrongly. ☐ B
   C She thinks all bureaucrats are inefficient. ☐ C

3 Why does the caller mention that her candidate needed the certificate?
   A She is ashamed because she failed to register her candidate. ☐ A
   B She thinks it's a possible way of persuading the clerk to make an exception to the rule. ☐ B
   C She is appealing to the clerk's feelings. ☐ C

4 Why does the caller get impatient?
   A She realises the clerk isn't going to make an exception. ☐ A
   B She begins to feel the system is against her. ☐ B
   C She thinks that if she's aggressive she may get what she wants. ☐ C

5 Why does the caller finally lose her temper?
   A She is angry about the clerk's accusation. ☐ A
   B She thinks the clerk is stupid for misunderstanding her. ☐ B
   C She thinks it's very unjust that she and her candidate will suffer for a mistake that wasn't theirs. ☐ C

Speaking

● **Questions on the photographs**

1 Describe the people in these pictures.
2 Describe their facial expressions and the
  way they are standing.
3 What do you think they are waiting for?
4 (*Pair work*) Interview one of the people. Ask
  him/her how long they have been waiting.
5 Where do you think each of these photos was
  taken? How do you know?
6 Do you get very annoyed when you have to
  queue up for something?
7 What other sorts of things annoy you?

1 Do you suffer from stress?
2 What do you think people could do to avoid getting annoyed and feeling tense?
3 Answer the following questions. Can you tell from your answers what might cause your stress?
   a) Are you in good health?
   b) Do you talk about your problems regularly or keep quiet?
   c) Do you smoke and drink a lot?
   d) Do you take regular exercise? How often?
   e) Are you seriously worried about your job?
   f) Are you a person who finds comfort in your religion?
   g) Do you often do things just for fun?
   h) Do you usually sleep eight hours every night?
   i) Are you a regular member of a social club?
   j) How much tea or coffee do you drink?

● Speech situation

Look through this short speech, answer the questions that follow and then discuss it.

Well, we turned up at the airline desk at the right time, in fact with time to spare. And the man said, quite happily, 'Oh, the Rome flight? Sorry, it's been cancelled.' And I said, 'What do you mean, it's been cancelled?' And he seemed to think that was funny, and said, 'It's been cancelled. Sorry.' And that made me *angry*. And I said, 'What are you going to do about us then? We've got a ticket to travel with your airline to Rome.' And he smiled and said he was sorry again. As if that was enough.

1 What incident is the speaker referring to?
2 What was the attitude of the man that the speaker is talking about?
3 How does the speaker feel about the incident?

● Role-play — group work

Work in groups of three. You share a flat together and you are having problems with your neighbours upstairs. First, work out individually what you would most like to complain about, then discuss your complaints and decide what you are going to do.

Individual choice

Listening

● **Pre-listening activity — pair work**

Find out what your partner's favourite television programmes are and why. Find out what he/she thinks of television in general.

● **Exercise 1**

You will hear three people talking about television programmes they watched last night. Look at the lists of programmes below and put the number 1, 2 or 3 in the right-hand column next to the programme that each speaker mentions. Put number 1 for the programmes that Speaker 1 mentions, number 2 for Speaker 2 and number 3 for Speaker 3.

TV

BBC 1

7.00 ICE SKATING. The St Ivel Gala of World Champions, with that golden pair who've covered themselves with glory, Christopher Dean and Jayne Torvill.

7.50 GREAT LITTLE RAILWAYS. Last in the series, with a railway line that sounds like a Big Dipper – the Guayaquil-Quito in Ecuador, 280 miles of switchbacks and loops that climb nearly 11,000 feet.

8.30 TEARS BEFORE BEDTIME. A new comedy series by Richard Waring about a mature couple who get fed up with their three teenage kids, and run away from home. Geraldine "Miss Brodie" McEwan and Francis Matthews are the liberated couple who see redundancy as a chance to escape the bedlam of home. Inspired by a true story apparently.

9.00 NEWS. WEATHER.

9.25 PLAY FOR TODAY. Atlantis. From the droll pen of Peter Terson, this is a one-off play that looks a natural to turn into a long-running comedy series.
The central characters are a couple of disenchanted assembly line mechanics, who decide to seek the fulfilment of their dreams by buying a canal boat and sailing off into the wild blue yonder.

10.40 PEOPLE AND POWER. The Foreign Secretary talks to David Dimbleby

about the world's economic problems.

11.23 NEWS HEADLINES.

11.25 BALLROOM CHAMPIONS. From the Hammersmith Palais, London.

12.10- 12.15 a.m. WEATHER, CLOSE.

BBC 2

7.30 NEWS

7.35 FILM: The War Of The Worlds (1953). An updated version of the H. G. Wells story about Martians causing havoc when they invade our planet. The special effects are more impressive than the efforts of the cast, which includes Gene Barry and Ann Robinson.

9.00 RUSSELL HARTY. With the kids from 'Fame'.

9.30 JUST ANOTHER DAY. Another of reporter John Pitman's absorbing forays into everyday life. This time he spends the day in Selfridges, the London department store which employs 3,000. It's just like 'Are You Being Served' he says.

10.00 DEAR LADIES. That dreadful pair Hinge and Bracket in another sharply-observed story of village life. The coming bowls match causes some excitement especially since there seems to be a shortage of umpires – until Dame Hilda rolls up her sleeves and prepares to step in.

10.30 NEWSNIGHT.

11.30- 12.25 a.m. OPEN UNIVERSITY.

ITV

7.00 REPORTING LONDON. The latest news from the capital.

7.35 FILM: Birds of Prey (1973). Made-for-TV movie starring David 'The Fugitive' Janssen as a helicopter pilot who tries his hand at a spot of detection work when he sees bank robbers making a quick getaway with a hostage.

9.00 STUDIO. Part two of a so-so serial about a recording studio, with the sinister manager Manville throwing his weight around tonight.

10.00 ITN NEWS. THAMES NEWS.

10.30 THE WOMAN AT NO. 10. Fascinating insight into the mind of Maggie in conversation with her old friend, novelist and guru, Sir Laurens van der Post. She talks about her childhood, her early interest in politics, how she met Denis, her role as a mother and religion.

11.30 MANNIX. Our hero races to the rescue of a young widow whose husband was killed by a car bomb.

12.20 a.m. IN HIS IMAGE? Ex-Hell's Angel Brian Greenaway talks to Frances Donnelly about his Christian faith.

12.30 CLOSE.

TV

CHANNEL 4

7.00 CHANNEL 4 NEWS.

7.50 COMMENT. Another personal view on a topical subject.

8.00 BROOKSIDE. Birthday celebrations for Bobby – but Damon and Karen have gone AWOL. Meanwhile Lucy and Gordon plan Easter in the Wirral.

8.30 FOR WHAT IT'S WORTH. Last in the series of excellent consumer programmes that investigates a wide range of items on offer, with David Stafford and Penny Junor.

9.00 FILM: The Day of the Locust (1974). An insight of the cruel reality that lies behind the glittering exterior of Hollywood. Karen Black plays a small-part actress and the chaps who fall for her are portrayed by Donald Sutherland and William Atherton. It's adapted from the novel by Nathanael West and directed by John Schlesinger.

11.35 BLACK ON BLACK. The latest news and opinions from black people in Britain and around the world plus the newest sounds in music, theatre and art. Beverley Anderson is the presenter.

12.25 a.m. CLOSE.

● **Exercise 2**

Listen to the following street interview on the subject of television viewing habits. Look at the interviewer's questionnaire below and complete it with the information you hear.

UNIVERSITY OF BLACKHEATH SOCIOLOGY DEPARTMENT/TELEVISION PROJECT

PERSON INTERVIEWED   Age...............   Occupation.......................

First name.........................   Surname..........................

1) On average, how many hours of television watched per week? Less than 4☐ 4-10☐ 11-20☐ More than 20☐

2) Does he/she usually plan viewing in advance to fit in with other things? (e.g. seeing friends/going to the cinema). YES/NO

3) Is he/she satisfied with television in general? Yes, very☐ Yes☐ Not sure☐ No☐

4) What sort of programmes does he/she like watching most?
News☐ Documentaries☐ Plays☐ Drama series☐ Comedy series☐
Films☐ Sport☐ Music☐ Shows☐ Others☐

5) What is the single best programme or series he/she has ever seen?
....

6) What is the single worst programme or series he/she has ever seen?
....

7) Which channel does he/she watch most?
BBC 1☐ BBC 2☐ ITV☐ Channel 4☐

8) Does he/she watch breakfast television? If so, BBC or ITV? ....

9) Does he/she watch Channel 4? If so for what? ....

10) Does television stop him/her   a) Reading?☐   b) Going to the cinema?☐   c) Going to the theatre?☐
d) Listening to the radio?☐

11) Does television reduce his/her social life?   YES/NO

12) Television and children :
a) Does he/she think parents should control the television watching habits of their children?   YES/NO
b) Does he/she think children learn a lot from television?   YES/NO

Speaking

● **Questions on the photographs**

Photograph 1

1 Look at the photograph and describe it in detail.
2 Where do you think it was taken? How do you know?
3 Can you describe the sort of clothes these boys are wearing?
4 What does their clothing tell you about the school?
5 Can you see any girls? Why not?
6 What do these children appear to think of the photographer?

Photograph 2

1 Look at the photograph and describe it in detail.
2 Describe the posture, clothing, facial expressions of the children.
3 What do you think that building in the background is?
4 What sort of school do you think this might be? How do you know?

Both photographs

(*Pair work*) Imagine one of the boys from picture 1 meets one of the boys from picture 2. Invent a conversation between them.

1 Do you think the state should pay for schools? (Some/all/none?)
2 Describe the educational system in your country. Are there both private and state schools? Which is better? Why?
3 Do you think boys and girls should go to school together or separately?
4 Do you think boys and girls should receive a different education, or the same?
5 Are there any disadvantages in having very expensive schools for the children of the very rich?
6 Find out if anyone in the class has been to a boarding school (one where the children live away from home during the term time). Can you see any advantages or disadvantages in this system?
7 Do you think religion should be taught in schools? How?
8 If you were the Minister of Education, how would you begin to improve the educational system in your country?
9 How much is education the responsibility of the parents and how much of the teachers?

● Speech situation

Look through this short speech, answer the questions that follow and then discuss it.

You'd better be careful with 5B. They're at an age when they can be... how shall I put it?... rather difficult to control. Normally, you'll find they'll be all right with you, I'm sure, because you only get them once a week, in small groups. But what I mean is, it's probably better for you not to be too... too *friendly* with them, because if you are, they may take advantage of you.

1 What does the passage refer to?
2 Where do you think this situation is taking place?
3 Who is warning whom?
4 What advice or warning does the speaker give?

● Talking point

Work in groups of three. First, individually, note down your answer to the following question and then discuss your ideas with your partners.
   How do you think education will change in the next twenty years?

Bad luck

Listening

● **Pre-listening activity — pair work**

Find out what experience your partner has had of losing things, leaving things behind or having things lost on planes, etc.

● **Exercise 1**

You will hear a conversation between an airline clerk and a passenger who has lost some of his luggage. Look at the lost property report below and complete it with the details that you hear about the lost luggage.

TRANSYLVANIAN AIRLINES

LOST PROPERTY REPORT

TIME _____

DATE _____

FLIGHT _____

COMING FROM _____

DESCRIPTION|OF LOST ITEM _____

MAKE OR DISTINGUISHING MARK _____

CONTENTS _____

● **Exercise 2**

This exercise is in two parts. In Part One of this exercise you will hear someone reporting to the police all the things that have been stolen from her house. Look at the pictures below and put a tick against the objects she mentions.

In Part Two of this exercise you will hear a police constable reporting to the inspector back at the police station on some items that he thinks may be stolen property. Look at the pictures and put a cross against the items he mentions.

1

2

3

4
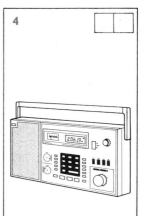

5

6

7

8

9

10

11

12

Speaking

● Questions on the photographs

Photograph 1

1 Describe the picture in detail.
2 What kind of place is this?
3 What can you see? Name the objects and describe the state they are in.
4 What do you think has happened? How do you know?
5 What do you think this man thought when he opened the door?
6 (*Pair work*) Act out an interview between a police officer and the man.
7 How could all this have been avoided?
8 What should the man have done? What shouldn't he have done?

Photograph 2

1 Describe the place and the objects.
2 Describe the people and the expressions on their faces.
3 What exactly has happened here?
4 Look at the tree and the wall. How exactly did this happen?
5 Do you think these people have anything to do with the car? Why?
6 (*Pair work*) Act out an interview between a police officer and the woman.
7 How could this have been avoided?
8 What should the driver have done? What shouldn't he have done?

Related topics

1 How can accidents be avoided?
2 Where do most accidents take place?
3 What sort of accidents most frequently occur in the home, in factories, in schools?
4 Find out if anyone in the class has had an accident. How could it have been avoided?
5 Have you ever been burgled? Tell the class about it. What did you feel like?
6 How, in general, can burglary be stopped?
7 Why do people steal things? How many different reasons can you think of?
8 Should people who steal things from their place of work be punished? How?
9 How are thieves and robbers punished? Is this a good idea?
10 What are the disadvantages of the prison system? Can you think of any alternatives?

● Speech situation

Look through this short speech, answer the questions that follow and then discuss it.

Don't worry, don't worry. Let's just go back over things. Now you last saw him when you were over there, in the electrical department, did you? Now if we start from there, and just look around... he may not have gone far, you know... they're very often just curious. They just wander off for a second then come back. Now, what exactly were you buying? I mean, which counter were you standing at?

1 Where do you think this situation is taking place?
2 What incident has just happened?
3 Who is speaking to whom?
4 How would you describe the speaker's manner towards the person spoken to?

● Prepared talk

Work individually at first. Prepare a brief (1–2 minute) talk on any topic related to *either* crime *or* accidents, and then give the talk to your partners. Here are some suggestions:

Do you think prisons should be comfortable?
Is poverty a major cause of crime?
Do you believe in capital punishment?

Test papers

Test 1

● **Listening comprehension**

First part 🔲

For each of the questions 1–5 put a tick (√) in one of the boxes A, B, C or D.

1 Julie is against travelling on the 8.00 train because

  A on that train there would be no cheap tickets.   ☐ A

  B the company are not paying their travel expenses.   ☐ B

  C they would have to leave home very early to catch it.   ☐ C

  D that train wouldn't arrive in Aberdeen until 6.00.   ☐ D

2 Rob doesn't want to go to Aberdeen by plane because

  A it's far too expensive.   ☐ A

  B the service between London and Aberdeen isn't very frequent.   ☐ B

  C he thinks it's dangerous.   ☐ C

  D for some reason he doesn't like flying.   ☐ D

3 Rob's main objection to travelling by overnight coach seems to be

  A he wouldn't be able to sleep at all because of the stops.   ☐ A

  B it isn't much cheaper than the train anyway.   ☐ B

  C he's worried about arriving late for the interview.   ☐ C

  D it would be uncomfortable to be sitting for so long.   ☐ D

4 Julie thinks the rail company offers 'day-saver' tickets because

  A they are only available on unpopular routes.   ☐ A

  B they want people to travel when trains are not normally full.   ☐ B

  C they want to encourage business people to travel at midday.   ☐ C

  D they want to make people think all trains are cheap.   ☐ D

5 Julie wants to travel overnight because

  A the journey takes less time.   ☐ A

  B it would give them time to prepare for the interview in the morning.   ☐ B

  C two nights in hotels would make the trip very expensive.   ☐ C

  D the company might pay travel expenses if they don't stay in any hotels.   ☐ D

Second part 🔊

*Fill in the information you hear on the notepad
below.*

1. HOW MANY YEARS FLYING JUMBOS?

2. NUMBER OF PASSENGERS A JUMBO CAN CARRY?

3. AGE OF PILOT?

4. NUMBER OF HOURS' FLYING HE HAS EVERY MONTH?

5. DO PILOTS GET A CHOICE OF ROUTES?

6. HOW OFTEN DOES A PILOT GET A MEDICAL CHECKUP?

7. HOW OFTEN DOES HE GET AN EYE CHECKUP?

8. TOTAL NUMBER OF PEOPLE IN A JUMBO CREW?

9. HOW MANY CREW ACTUALLY RESPONSIBLE FOR FLYING PLANE?

10. HOW OFTEN DOES JUMBO GET 24-HOUR INSPECTION?

11. HOW OFTEN DOES A PLANE GET A COMPLETE SERVICE CHECK?

12. TOTAL NUMBER OF PILOT'S FLYING HOURS?

Third part

Put a tick, as shown in No. 1, against each picture which shows the sleeping positions mentioned.

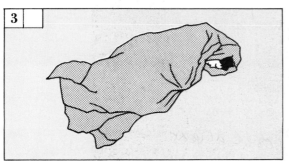

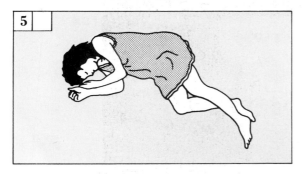

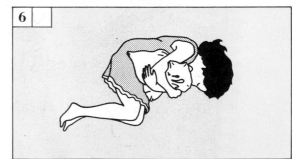

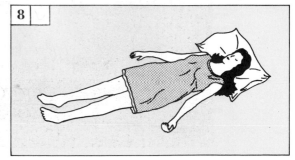

(i) *Look at this picture carefully and be prepared to answer some questions about it.*

1 What are the boys doing in the photograph?
2 Where do you think they are?
3 How old do you think they may be?
4 Describe their appearance.
5 Are the machines in the picture allowed in your country? If they are, has there been any campaign to have them banned?

Suggest better ways of spending spare time.

Talk about any hobby of yours.

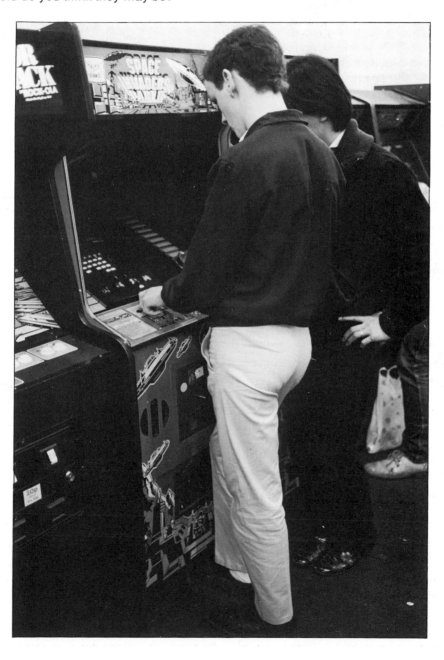

(ii) *Look at this passage and be prepared to answer some questions about it and then to discuss it.*

The best way, the very best way to dig, you know, is to get someone else to do it for you, if you can. But there's no way out of digging, if you want things to grow. Autumn's a good time for it, before the weather gets too cold. But don't dig when the soil's really wet, when it's heavy, or you'll do yourself an injury.

1 What is this passage about?
2 Who is the advice meant for?
3 What are the best conditions for doing the work described?

(iii) *There may be a variety of options offered in this section. Choose one of the following.*

a) Briefly take time to make notes on *one* of the following topics, and then give a brief (half-a-minute or so) talk to the class/group. When you finish, they can ask you questions.
1 My favourite memory of school.
2 Advertising.
3 The advantages of living in a flat, rather than a house.

b) You are travelling in an English-speaking country with a friend, when the friend gets ill with a severe headache and a high temperature. Act out the conversation you might have with the local chemist, in the following stages.
1 Explain the problem/symptoms.
2 Ask what the chemist would recommend.
3 Talk about the medicine with the chemist.
4 Ask about a local doctor.
5 Pay for the medicine and thank the chemist.

Test 2

● Listening comprehension

First part 🔲.

*Put a tick, as shown in No. 1, against each
piece of advice given.*

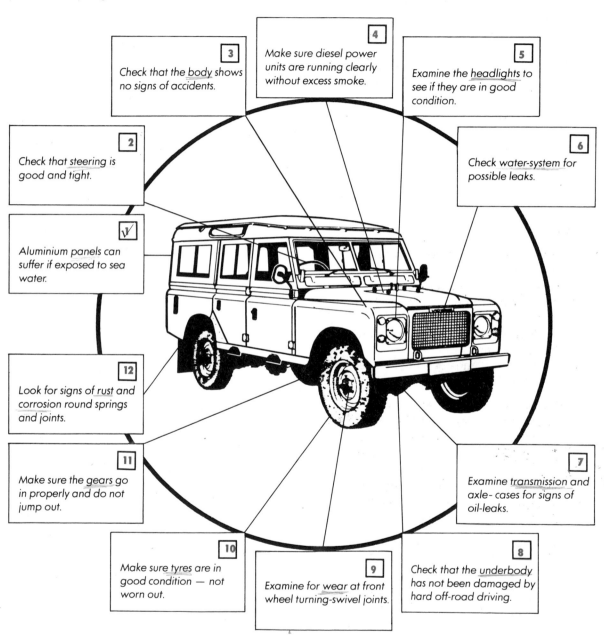

3 Check that the body shows no signs of accidents.

4 Make sure diesel power units are running clearly without excess smoke.

5 Examine the headlights to see if they are in good condition.

2 Check that steering is good and tight.

6 Check water-system for possible leaks.

✓ Aluminium panels can suffer if exposed to sea water.

12 Look for signs of rust and corrosion round springs and joints.

11 Make sure the gears go in properly and do not jump out.

7 Examine transmission and axle-cases for signs of oil-leaks.

10 Make sure tyres are in good condition — not worn out.

9 Examine for wear at front wheel turning-swivel joints.

8 Check that the underbody has not been damaged by hard off-road driving.

Second part

For each of the questions 1–4, put a tick (√) in one of the boxes A, B, C or D.

1 Sally's mother
  A spends any money Sally gives her on a housekeeper.   A ☐
  B insists that Sally should help with the housework.   B ☐
  C feels Sally has no need to pay anything at all.   C ☐
  D prefers that Sally should help with the housework.   D ☐

2 At first, Sally's father
  A encouraged her interest in video games.   A ☐
  B forbade her completely to go near video games.   B ☐
  C got her a job in a pet shop to pay for her video interest.   C ☐
  D didn't approve of her playing video games at all.   D ☐

3 Sally
  A must already have been keen on computers while she was in the pet shop.   A ☐
  B took a computer programming course with the company.   B ☐
  C does her best work at home late at night.   C ☐
  D doesn't really write the programs at all.   D ☐

4 Sally's father
  A doesn't think bus-driving is a very hard job.   A ☐
  B advises Sally to make the best of success while it lasts.   B ☐
  C thinks Sally's high salary shows how stupid video game players are.   C ☐
  D says Sally must be very clever to be able to write computer programs.   D ☐

Third part

*Look at the questions below. When you hear the answer to the questions on the tape, write the **number of the question** against the appropriate time(s) in the answer. No. 1 is done for you.*

1 When is the best time to go to the dentist?
2 When are the body and mind in their best condition at the same time?
3 When does the body feel pain most?
4 And when does it feel pain least?
5 When is the worst time to work?
6 And when is the best time to study something difficult?
7 At what time of day does the body use up less energy?
8 What is a bad time for restless sleepers?

a.m.		p.m.	
0000 – 0100		1200 – 1300	
0100 – 0200		1300 – 1400	
0200 – 0300		1400 – 1500	
0300 – 0400		1500 – 1600	
0400 – 0500		1600 – 1700	1
0500 – 0600		1700 – 1800	
0600 – 0700		1800 – 1900	
0700 – 0800		1900 – 2000	
0800 – 0900		2000 – 2100	
0900 – 1000		2100 – 2200	
1000 – 1100		2200 – 2300	
1100 – 1200		2300 – 2400	

(i) *Look at this picture carefully and be
prepared to answer some questions about
it.*

1 Describe the people you see in this
photograph.
2 Whose parents do you think the older
couple are?
3 From the house and surroundings, what
sort of life do you think these people
lead?
4 How do you think each person in the
picture feels about the new baby?
5 Who do you think took the photograph?
6 What do you think the little girl on the
right is looking at?

Changes in family life in your country
during the last 25 years.
Advantages and disadvantages of families
living close together.

(ii) *Look at this passage and be prepared to
answer some questions about it and then
to discuss it.*

No, I wouldn't take it from there, if I were
you. Why don't you have a look from here?
You get a much better view, you know. All
right, don't then, but don't say I didn't tell
you. But really, if you came back here, to
where I am, you'd get the whole building in,
and the garden at the front.

1 What is happening in the passage?
2 Where might it be taking place?
3 What is the attitude of the speaker to the
person spoken to?

(iii) *There may be a variety of options offered in this section. Choose one of the following.*

a) By surprise, three generations of a family who are great friends of your parents' arrive at your home one Sunday afternoon when you are alone and the rest of your family will not be back for at least three hours. What would you do to keep the group amused till then?

b) Make up a brief definition of:
an umbrella
a hammer
a dry-cleaner's
make-up.

Briefly, what do you think of:
ice-cream
zoos
computers
self-service restaurants.

c) You and a friend are on holiday in an English-speaking country and you see an advertisement for a cheap coach-tour holiday in a part of that country that you both want to visit. Work out the conversation you might have in the travel agency with the agency clerk. You want to know:
possible dates and times of departures;
real costs (any hidden extra expenses?);
what is included in the price;
what kind of hotels are used by the agency;
how much free time you will get to visit places;
if a guide is included;
if the guide will speak your language.